The Optimism of Butler's 'Analogy'

HENRY SCOTT HOLLAND

1908

TABLE OF CONTENTS

THE OPTIMISM OF BUTLER'S ANALOGY

THE OPTIMISM OF BUTLER'S ANALOGY

The great and memorable statesman who devoted the overflowing energies of his leisure hours to the delivery of the first Romanes Lecture consecrated all the force of his last years of life, after his public career was closed, to an effort at recalling the attention of the world of thought to the significance of Bishop Butler.

He had grown to intellectual stature in the days when the influence of Butler had been for Oxford a sacred and inspiring inheritance. It stood for all that was manly, massive, and profound. It entered into the character and the life, as an abiding possession. 'About this time,' says J. H. Newman in the Apologia, 'I read Bishop Butler's Analogy, the study of which has been to so many, as it was to me, an era in their religious opinions.' That is a judgement characteristic of the time—a judgement which Mr. Gladstone would have adopted with whole-hearted ardour. And it was to him a deep and inexplicable wonder that such a judgement should have become strange and obsolete in the intellectual atmosphere of his own University. He could not tolerate or forgive the dismissal of Butler from his place of honour in the Philosophical School: nor could he understand how the younger generation could have suffered him to lapse out of their intellectual horizons. Indignantly, he toiled to repair the wrong. The weight of eighty years could not hold him back. To the very last moment of his working life, before he passed under the bitter discipline of pain in the very antechamber of death itself, he nursed the unconquerable hope, and brooded over the cause to which his soul was committed. He gave us an edition of Bishop Butler which for the first time made his works presentable and attractive. He edited; he assorted; he prefaced; he added subsidiary studies. He offered us the opportunity of reconsideration. He challenged us to say whether we were prepared to let the great tradition die.

That challenge has been made, as yet, in vain. It has roused no concern; it has evoked no new examination of Butler's claims to philosophical importance. His work remains still outside the current of living speculation.

Is it worth while, then, to go back on an issue that has been decided? The case has been made with incomparable force, under unique conditions of power and pathos; and the verdict has been adverse. Who can be presumptuous enough to repeat an experiment which has received already such an august and final dismissal?

No one, indeed, would dare it, if it was a matter which depended on personal qualifications. But that is, mercifully, not the case. The conditions which determine the doctrine and the concentration of the intellectual interests of an Age lie far beyond the range of personal influence. They lie back in the secret motions of organic growth; in the subtle processes of mental transformation; in the massed and manifold experiences which go to the creation of a social speculative temperament. There is a structure of living thought for ever in making, through infinite reaction on its environment, and in touch with a special atmosphere. To it, individuals are but accidental. It holds in itself its own principle of advance, and grows by the law of its own growth. Our highest function is to co-operate with its movement; to do our minute contributory work within its encompassing influence. We cannot force it. We know but dimly the springs on which it draws; the hidden source from which it derives its momentum. We can but lend ourselves to become the instruments through which it achieves its own peculiar process of intellectual assimilation.

And it is because there is so much in our immediate situation which appears to me to be in sympathetic touch with the peculiar qualities of Butler's mind, that I am emboldened to believe that, by the ordinary and natural movement of thought, and not through any individual plea raised on his behalf, the moment is arrived in which he may, once again, be drawn into the central currents of our intellectual life.

But, if this, is to happen, it can only be done through a bold and drastic abandonment of much that stands in the way of his recognition as a modern constructive force.

First, as we all know, the particular Controversy, in which he was mainly engaged, is wholly dead and done with. The Deist, with whom he was concerned, was the special product of a certain temporary stage of scientific development. He was the normal intellectual deposit of the great mechanical Sciences. Under the infinite elasticity of mathematical categories, Physics and Astronomy had given to man's apprehension of the Universe an amazing expansion. For the first time, he had grasped something of its appalling scale. Yet, even in his minute insignificance, he had the faculty to recognize the reign of intelligent Law; and in this intelligibility of Law, in this rational Order and Design, governing every part with mechanical accuracy, directing the whole according to a preconceived scheme, he saw the evidence of a God who answered to his own rationality. The Religion of the living heart, of romance, of pathos, of tragedy, might have to vanish, in face of this absorbing and abstract mechanism. Christianity ceased to have a meaning; because man's emotional life in the flesh, here on earth, had ceased to have any value. Such a life with its passions and its desires, its laughter and its tears, would not fall into mathematical categories. And it fled away into ashamed nothingness before the hosts that peopled the enormous heavens. But the God of Design and Purpose, who responded to the demands of pure reason, remained on His throne. Religion survived in the form of Deism.

So it might succeed in doing, in that brief moment when Science was mainly mathematical and abstract in type. But the development that followed took an entirely novel direction. The Sciences of Life took up the running. Interest passed from mechanism to biology. And, with this change of interest, a wholly new scientific ideal began to dominate our intellectual imagination. It was the ideal of growth. Life was in movement. That was its fascination. It evolved; it changed; it pushed its advance; it acted; it reacted; it acquired; it assimilated; it strove and strained; it knew no rest. The closer men drew to this wonderful and stirring secret, the less were they able to abide contented with the motionless fixities of the more abstract mechanical formularies. The immanent reality of the Universe is not to be found in the cold exhibition of changeless, mathematical law, but in the infinite diversities of a living and growing organism. The Universe is a vast, dramatic experiment. At its base is volcanic energy, holding in itself infinite potentialities, which storm their way into gradual realization, and under the terrible processes of unceasing strife, by efforts which are often effectual by the very blindness of their insistent stress, work out their fitness to survive. Such was the picture which Science unveiled.

And in such a Universe, the poor Deist found no footing. After all, his Christian opponent, with his passion for life, his gospel of growth, his romantic emotionalism, his central Tragedy, his bloody struggle through Death to Life, was more in touch and tune with this new gospel of evolution, than he, with his abstract intellectualism and 'bloodless categories'. The rational Deist was harder hit than any one by the scientific developments of the nineteenth century.

And, with his disappearance, we may suffer the whole method of the controversy to vanish too. Superficially, it wore, always, a most unfortunate and repellent air. It looked so meticulous and arid. It was apt to feel like a mere 'tu quoque', which irritated even if it silenced. It developed the dilemma, 'Either accept my position, or abandon yours'; and nobody was ever convinced of anything by a dilemma. Its outward appearance wholly belied the real constructive grounds which lay behind it. And these can only be seen in their full worth by sweeping away the dialectical superstructure which hides them from view.

For, of course, the reading of Butler could never have made an epoch in anybody's life, such as Newman typically felt it to be, if he had actually rested his case on what W. H. Simcox named the 'argumentum ad horribile'. The Tractarians were the last people who would have been deeply moved by a logical acuteness which simply convicted the Deist of having as difficult a cause to justify as any Christian. So long as that is all that we see in the Analogy, we have failed to account for everything that the name of Butler stood for with those whom he most deeply swayed.

What, then, is the secret of the profound impression that he made? It is this which we would try to detach and to rehearse. And, first, as an index of the influence he wielded, what can be more noticeable than the passage in the familiar Preface prefixed to the Analogy by Bishop Halifax, in which he traces to the quotation from the Son of Sirach the germ of the entire work? 'All things are double one against another; and God hath made nothing imperfect.' 'On this single observation,' the Bishop writes, 'the whole fabric of our prelate's defence of Religion is based.'

We can recognize, in this assertion, the temper and companionship with which Butler was associated by his friends.

There is no idea of attributing to him the dialectical success of a cynical Pessimist, impaling opponents on the horns of some futile dilemma. The 'argumentum ad horribile' is utterly ignored. Rather, his admirers were led to recognize his close affinities with that intellectual companionship which, under the sanction of the Solomonic tradition, devoted itself to the high service of our Lady Wisdom, its Mistress and Queen. There, in that brave and confident movement, in which Hellenic width of outlook was combined with the practical securities of the concrete Hebraistic mind, they recognized the mould in which Butler's thinking was fashioned. And, in this recognition, they witness to the breadth of scope, the wide horizon, the confident patience, the delicate appreciation of graduated purpose, which they associate with his name.

For, indeed, this phrase from the Son of Sirach is the typical expression of the ancient optimism which saw, everywhere, the evidence of that Wisdom which 'goeth from end to end, and sweetly ordereth all things'. It belongs to a school of thought which is supremely sure of man's capacity to enter into his intellectual heritage, and to move freely in that large air. It is not the preacher of vanity and agnosticism with whom we are concerned. The note struck is full of hope, and of assurance. It tells of a Wisdom of God, who invites all men to share in her riches—calling to them at the comers of the streets, in the chief places of concourse, in the opening of the gates: 'For she goeth about seeking such as are worthy of her, showeth herself favourably unto them in the ways, and meeteth them in every thought' (Wisd. vi). 'She preventeth them that desire her, in making herself first known unto them. Yea, she is easily seen of them that love her, and found of such as seek her. For Wisdom is more moving than any motion: she passeth through all things by reason of her pureness.' 'For in her is an understanding spirit, holy, one only, manifold, subtil, lively, clear, loving the thing that is good, kind to man, steadfast, sure, free from care, having all power, overseeing all things, and going through all understanding, pure, and most subtil spirits, in all ages entering into holy souls, and making them friends of God' (Wisd. vii).

Was there ever a nobler and purer manifestation of the passion for Intellectual Truth? Did optimistic belief in human faculties ever go beyond this strong assurance?

And Butler seemed to his fellows to belong to this company: to hold their faith; to be transfigured by their vision. In all that he wrote, he was looking at Nature with their eyes, and worked in the magnificence of their impulse. He raised his whole fabric of defence on their basic thought of a comprehensive and delicate wisdom which 'setteth all things in balance', 'double one against another.' He was fascinated by their portrayal of a world that was ordered throughout, under the secure certainties of unfailing law; in which everything was measured, placed, ordained, established, by virtue of infinite relationships that bound it up into a Whole, which was continuous, rational, coherent. The closer we look into this literature of the Wisdom, the nearer we seem to draw to the inspiration that speaks to us in phrase after phrase of the Analogy, and to the temper, the mood, the judgement, the insight, which create its characteristic atmosphere. As we ponder over the old refrains, we seem to catch Bishop Butler at work; we feel ourselves to be inside the process of thought by which he arrived at his special and dominant formulae. We can see how he absorbed their far-reaching justification of a world in which 'All the works of the Lord were good'—'good,' that is, in their place; at their season; at the last: good, if we could only understand their purpose. 'None can say, What is this? wherefore is that? for at time convenient they shall all be sought out. The Lord seeth from everlasting to everlasting; and there is nothing wonderful before Him.' So the Son of Sirach wrote of old. And can we not hear Butler repeating it after him? Did he not take on his own lips the strong resolution of this Son of Sirach: 'Therefore from the beginning I was resolved, and thought upon these things, and have left them in writing. All the works of the Lord are good: and He will give every needful thing in due season. So that a man cannot say, This is worse than that: for in time they shall all be well approved' (Ecclus. xxxix). 'All these things live and remain for ever for all uses, and they are all obedient. All things are double one against another:

and He hath made nothing imperfect. One thing establisheth the good of another: and who shall be filled with beholding His glory?' (Ecclus. xlii).

Surely Bishop Halifax has read Butler aright. The echoes of these announcements reverberate throughout the Analogy.

And the special phrase, that he has selected as typical, has a peculiar bearing upon Butler's own speculative mood. 'All things are double one against another.' It suggests that not only does the world offer the spectacle of unbroken and changeless Law; but, always, there is a sense of repetition in the sequence. The same rhythms reappear, as the mind passes sweetly from end to end of the long order. Again and again, Creation follows a Leit-motif; repeats a phrase; recurs to some normal programme. There are methodical formalities which lie at the base of all the measureless variety of effects; and these are recaptured, by the imagination, at each stage, on every level, in each department, of life. It is as if Nature had that delight that was so characteristic of Beethoven, of developing all the fertility of variation that can be wrung out of a single simple theme. Wherever you pass, throughout these infinite gradations of natural development, you seem to be reiterating the one formula which expresses the innermost secret of all growth: 'First the blade, then the ear, then the full corn in the ear.' Materials change; possibilities vary indefinitely according to the level of the domain with which you may be concerned; but something in the method is ever identical. In each new experience, you find yourself on familiar ground. A resemblance holds; a memory haunts; a harmony links; a note is struck of association and similarity.

'All things are double one against another.' So the Son of Sirach said. And so, most certainly, Butler deeply felt. His main strength comes out in his exhibition of the intense and intimate famillarities which recur in the working of the Divine Purpose, wherever you encounter it. It retains always the same style; it displays always the same mind; it holds fast to its own identity, under every variety of condition and circumstance. Always, the like effects follow from the like causes. Always, the contrasted departments of activity reveal a strangely exact parallelism in their typical development.

So he delights in noting; and in this it is good to remember that we are on the traditional Gospel ground. We are travelling along the lines given us by Christ Himself. For we are but repeating, in a scientific form, the reality declared by all our Lord's Parables. These Parables, as we know, are not allegories. They simply interpret the law of life on the one plane by the law of life on another. It is not a matter of two laws that can be compared; but of one and the same law, acting in two directions, on different levels, through diverse material. Seen on the earthly plane, acting through physical material, the law of life manifests exactly the methods under which it works in the Kingdom of God, through spiritual instruments.

And, as with the Parables, so, also, it was with all the activities of our Lord.

If He concentrated His personal pressure on the sick body of one who had faith to admit His will into action, it rose and walked. If He concentrated the same personal pressure on a receptive soul, its sins were forgiven. That which happened in the one case was the same as what happened in the other. That which accounted for the one would equally account for the other. 'For all things are double one against another.'

Such is the truth delivered to us through the Gospel Record. And Butler had won firm hold of this dominating thought; and so it is that, under his direction, we find ourselves moving along a Universe which is an organic whole from end to end; and, ever as we shift our perspective or change our level, we become aware, by his help, of one and the same underlying secret. The same mind discloses itself; the same presence greets us; the same face looks out at us. This is the great principle of Analogy, by which (in the words of Bishop Halifax) 'he first inquires what the constitution of Nature, as made known to us in the way of experiment, actually is. And, from this, now seen and acknowledged, he endeavours to form a judgement of the larger constitution which religion discovers to us.' The emphasis so unhappily laid by the argument on the correspondence between objections and perplexities in the one case and in the other, obscures, by its dismal repugnance, our apprehension of the larger imaginative and constructive conception, on which the apologetic 'tu quoque' really rests. The correspondence in the character of the difficulties becomes for Butler an additional corroboration of his positive speculation. And it is this positive speculation which gives him his position as a thinker; not the merely incidental value, whatever it may be, of the minor controversial retort. For the force of the retort depends entirely on the primal conception of the intimate and essential correspondence that gives continuity to the two spheres of experience—a continuity which is recognized on its own account, and for its own impressive significance, quite apart from the accidental and additional confirmation of it which may, possibly, be derived from the discovery that, not only in its stable and elemental appeals to our intelligent confidence, but also even in its temporary obscurities, the same law of resemblance can be detected. No doubt, it is something to recognize that, even in these disagreeable misadventures, 'all things are double one against another.' But that is but a little or partial incident by the side of the splendid affirmation of universal coherence. 'Surely, it is of importance to learn,' says Bishop Halifax, 'that the natural and moral world are intimately connected, and are parts of one stupendous whole or system.'

The impression, then, made by Butler upon those who understood him best was that of a constructive and organic thinker. They felt the parallel between him and the Wisdom Literature. And as we note how instinctively the ancient phrases and terms reappear in his writing, we can be sure they were justified in doing so. But he, also, himself, by direct references to the influences under which he acted, implicated himself in a like alliance. For it was Origen, as everybody knows, who suggested to him the lines on which the Analogy runs. And the very sound of his name, as an ally, should have made it impossible for us to allow the Bishop to disguise himself as a sceptical pessimist, parading the depressing defects to which our reason has to submit. Origen's mind was architectonic. He built for knowledge a noble pleasure-house. He was optimistic to a fault. His range was immense. His power and wealth of imagination swept over the whole field of knowledge with unflagging energy. In him, all experience was drawn together under the mastery of a single Divine Purpose, into organic integrity, under the assimilating control of the Spirit, according to the methods of vital growth. He laboured to expand the scope of our speculation over the widest horizons, so as to embrace life in its richest fertilities, in its inexhaustible fullness. And he trusted to attain this magnificent consummation by confident use of the inspired and imaginative reason, which could, by mystical synthesis, transform and transcend the limitations of a narrow logic. And this is Butler's master. This is the source of his inspiration. It is under the influence of the famous phrase which the great Alexandrian supplied to him that the two worlds of Nature and Grace, of Experience and Spirit, of Reason and Revelation, are seen to be of one piece, of one type, of one purpose, illuminated by correspondences, interpreted by reiteration of a common theme, knit together into coherent sequence by kindred analogies, and delicate refrains, and responsive corroborations, and intimate resemblances, and recurring parallels.

Let us listen to his own weighty exposition of this prevailing theme. Cumbrous it is, and heavy-footed; the language strains under its load; its structure builds itself together by efforts that are apparent and undisguised; the colour and tone are subdued. We may feel, perhaps, the force of Walter Bagehot's jibe that no one would know from reading the Analogy, that the earth was not a square coal-pit. The arguments would all apply equally well.

Yet, in its very sense of effort, the passage has its literary effect. It conveys to the reader the bulk and volume of the over-mastering thought.

However, thus much is manifest, that the whole natural world and government of it is a scheme or system; not a fixed, but a progressive one; a scheme in which the operation of various means takes up a great length of time, before the ends they tend to can be attained. The change of seasons, the ripening of the fruits of the earth, the very history of a flower, is an instance of this; and so is human life. Thus vegetable bodies and those of animals, though possibly formed at once, yet grow up by degrees to a mature state. And thus rational agents, who animate these latter bodies, are naturally directed to form each his own manners and character, by the gradual gaining of knowledge and experience, and by a long course of action. Our existence is not only successive, as it must be of necessity; but one state of our life and being is appointed by God, to be a preparation for another; and that, to be the means of attaining to another succeeding one: infancy to childhood; childhood to youth; youth to mature age. Men are impatient, and for precipitating things; but the Author of nature appears deliberate throughout his operations; accomplishing his natural ends by slow successive steps. And there is a plan of things beforehand laid out, which, from the nature of it, requires various systems of means, as well as length of time, in order to the carrying on its several parts into execution. Thus, in the daily course of natural providence, God operates in the very same manner as in the dispensation of Christianity; making one thing subservient to another; this, to somewhat further; and so on, through a progressive series of means, which extend, both backward and forward, beyond our utmost view. Of this manner of operation, everything we see in the course of nature is as much an instance, as any part of the Christian dispensation (Anal. II. iv. 8).

After all, in this long-drawn labouring fashion, we are in direct touch with the poets of high vision. We are in the very mood which broods over the 'flower in the crannied wall'. We are close upon the 'Presence far more deeply interfused'.

It was natural enough that Cardinal Newman should have drawn from this analogy between two separate departments of God's work, the conclusion that 'the less important system is economically or sacramentally connected with the more momentous system'. For the sacramental conception of reality is, simply, the concrete expression of the law that 'all things are double one against another.' The physical reproduces the secret of the spiritual. The same ultimate verity realizes itself in a single act, under a double form. It is a matter of indifference under which term it is expressed; for the actuality is identical with itself on either level, in either sphere.

This sacramentalism agrees with what is known of Butler's ecclesiastical tendencies. But it is curiously characteristic of Cardinal Newman to have discovered in this sacramentalism which he learned from Butler a confirmation of his own boyish belief in the unreality of material phenomena. For this is the exact reverse of the consequence which Bishop Butler drew from his analogy. It is in direct contradiction with the impression under which he arrived at it.

And it is this that I desire to emphasize, with all the strength at my command. For it touches the very root of the matter.

Butler rested his whole argument upon the immediate and unquestioned reality of material phenomena and upon the validity of human experience. There, in the solid facts as they were felt, lay his ultimate appeal. They were his standard of certainty. They supplied him with his canon of secured knowledge, through which he could venture to make an advance towards other and higher regions which were more remote from experimental certification.

His entire scheme starts from this initial assumption. He is absolutely sure that we can observe facts, so that they are really known to us. And he prepares to argue from these common facts of experience, known in the way in which we act upon them in the ordinary pursuits of daily life, to others that are like them, which belong to the region of natural and revealed religion. He is convinced that there is a certain department of the divine government which comes, now, under our view. We are in possession of it, in our degree. We cover it, more or less. We understand some of its method and use. And it is because this present experience is so sure and real that we can trust the abstract reasoning which attempts the treatment 'of the larger and more general government which lies beyond our view'.

Yet, to our dismay, Butler disguises this, his robust confidence in experience, by selecting for it the most unlucky title that he could possibly have chosen. He gives to this effective certitude the nickname of 'probability'. And the name has haunted his reputation. It has left upon the world's casual memory the impression that he had no solid intellectual ground to offer us; and that he invited us to stake our souls on a chance. He figures, in popular imagination, as the respectable grey-haired old confederate in the crowd, who induces the bystander to take the odds on the hidden pea. He himself uses the unfortunate metaphor of stakes or odds at one moment in the argument, where he is illustrating his point from common experience. And, always, the word probability evokes the thought of dialectical ingenuity, rather than of massive reasoning. It is the Apologist that it recalls, not the Thinker. We feel, as we start off on an estimate of the convergent probabilities, as if we were to be captured by craft, drawn by subtle complications into a position for which we shall not be able wholly to account. Each separate bit of the evidence will be too weak to bear the strain of the great conclusion. Yet the accumulative effect of the inconclusive premises will compel us to assent to something more than they actually warrant. So we foresee; so it happens. We are sucked along. There is no precise moment at which we can pull up, and refuse to go further. We have no objection that we can make good. We cannot deny the pressure of the accumulation. Yet we have no instrument by which to test its exact validity. This type of process lands us in a discomfortable temper in which to face the Eternities. None of us like it. And it is this temper which is associated with Butler's argument from probability.

Now, it is difficult to imagine any temper so remote from what he intended to evoke. He is, in reality, appealing to the downright common-sense certitude with which the plain man accepts solid facts. He proves this by bringing as an instance of what he is thinking of, the expectation that the sun will rise to-morrow, and be seen, when it is seen at all, in the figure of a circle and not of a square. That expectation rests on probability, says Butler.

But that does not mean that the plain man is uncertain about the issue. To him, the fact that the sun is sure to rise is a type of all he means by certainty. It is for him the least improbable thing that he can think of. He cannot bring himself to doubt it. He would stake his life on it. Sun-rise, sun-setting—these embody the fixed immutabilities of Nature; they stand for the undeviating persistence of Physical Law; they are the fundamental basis on which he builds his experience as on a rock.

But why, then, identify this certitude with probability? Why call it by a name which so strongly belies its character?

Because Butler wants to drive it home to the plain man, that the convictions and the experiences on which he gaily and confidently grounds his most familiar actions are of a character which does not admit of logical proof. Tried by the standard of the metaphysician, they are mere probabilities. Yet they include the deepest motives of our being. They are sufficient to justify our most vital decisions. We fall back on them with a sense of absolute security. We act on them without a fear. Yes! and we are perfectly right, Butler would say. In all practical affairs we have no other way of acting.

And Religion is a practical affair. Religion is a problem of action. It is no metaphysic; it is a life. As action, as life, it conforms to all other types of life and action. It finds its certainties (that is) in what the metaphysician would condemn as probabilities. Religion is asking no more of you than your daily common practical experience does, when it invites you to trust to convictions that you cannot prove by syllogisms. It simply asks you to carry into its domain the same practical temper which avails you so well in all your earthly affairs.

Now, we can see the immense significance of this firm reliance on ordinary experience at the moment when Butler wrote. For it was the moment at which Natural Science was becoming the norm of certitude. It was beginning to assert the dominance that we know so well to-day, in determining the conditions which reason and imagination are prepared to accept as credible, and the certainties to which conduct is ready to conform. And Butler, by his confidence in experience, has already struck up an alliance with Natural Science. He has drawn it all over to his side in this matter of probability. For Science is merely an extension of this ordinary experience of ours over an immense area, by means of organized research into the multiplicity and variety of facts. And, if so, it submits to all the usual conditions of our practical experience. It depends on truths which it takes for granted. Its strongest certitudes are incapable of proof. They are what the metaphysicians would term probabilities. The real existence of its facts; the validity of our impressions of the facts; the value of convictions based on expectation, and derived from sheer force of habit and association; these are, for Science, its primal grounds, for which it offers no verification. It can only appeal to its own practical security of belief. On this it stands, and stands effectively. It ignores the metaphysical difficulties. They simply do not touch or affect it. It goes on, as if they were not there. And it is absolutely right to do so. It is dealing with facts; and it must take the facts as they are. It cannot, in its character as Science, go behind them, or vex itself with the preliminary problem, how there came to be any facts there at all for it to handle; or how it became aware of them and of its capacity to deal with them.

Only, if this is its own practical method of arriving at certainty, it cannot deny the right of Religion to use the same method. For Religion is a Science, a Science of fact. It claims that certain conditions are present and active, here and now; that certain things happen; that certain powers are at play; that certain possibilities are actually open; that a certain contact with the facts wins a certain response; that certain events, in this world of spiritual fact, have a real and direct bearing on man's life and behaviour. God has done certain things. To experience what He has done is Religion. These facts of the spiritual world are as coherent and solid as the facts of the natural world. And they are to be known in the same way. The principles, methods, and rules which hold good in the natural world will hold good here also. For both worlds are on the same lines. 'They are double one against the other.' Trust the same methods by which you have organized your natural experience, and they will justify themselves in this other department. Did you act there on gathered hints, on dim suggestions, on expectations, on tentative experiments, on implied correspondences, on a variety of converging probabilities which only grew into certainties as your experience took them up, and made ventures upon them, and found that, by the venture, it advanced? Is that the invariable type of your activities in contact with facts, in your natural existence? Well, then, why be surprised if you have to repeat exactly the like process in Religion; if here, too, you have to feel your way forward by hints, and suggestions, and experiments, and expectations, and probabilities? God is the same God, at whatever level of life you encounter Him. And always He will guide you by His eye, and not, as if you were a mule, by bit and bridle. Religion is no exception to what you already know so familiarly: it follows the same rule.

So Butler continually argues; and all the force of his mind comes out in this splendid confidence that he has in facts, in experience, in the validity of our faculties. He was no metaphysician. We feel this in the chapters on the Future Life, and on Necessity. He is here at his weakest. He fails to convince. He is not in his true atmosphere or element. He comes to himself, and to his full power, when he is flinging aside all the metaphysical problem which underlies life, as freely as the plain man does in practice, in daily experience, in science. Butler has no desire to taunt, when he convicts men of acting on probability. Far from it! He desires to emphasize the authoritative and justifiable character of such evidence: for, indeed, he needs it for his own purpose. He wishes to lend to the plain man in the street, and to the scientific man in the laboratory, his own robust assurance, his own unqualified belief, that in refusing to go behind the evidence and to question its validity, they and he were utterly and entirely in their right.

'It is not my design,' he says, 'to inquire further into the nature, the foundation, and the measure of probability,... or to guard against the errors to which reasoning from analogy is liable. This belongs to the subject of Logic, and is a part of that subject which has not yet been thoroughly considered. Indeed, I shall not take upon me to say how far the extent, compass, and force of analogical reasoning can be reduced to general heads and rules, and the whole be formed into a system. But though so little has been attempted in this way, by those who have treated of our intellectual powers, this does not hinder but that we may be, as we unquestionably are, assured that analogy is of weight, in various degrees, towards determining our judgement and our practice.... It is enough to the present purpose to observe that this general way of arguing is evidently natural, just, and conclusive. For there is no man can make a question but that the sun will rise to-morrow, and be seen, when it is seen, in the figure of a circle and not of a square' (Anal., Introduction, § 7).

This general way of arguing is eminently 'natural, just, and conclusive'. So he judges out of the heart of his buoyant optimism. Was there ever a firmer note of cheerful assurance in things as they are? It does not signify in the least that the logical justification lags hopelessly behind; that, indeed, it is far to seek; that the metaphysician is discharging all his artillery, with deadly precision, against the position taken, and is riddling it through and through. Butler does not care, any more than Physical Scientists care to-day, for the merciless demonstration of the futility of their primary grounds. They are convinced, as he was, that, whatever may be said, their way of arguing is eminently 'natural, just, and conclusive'. They would say with him, and with all the multitude of men who are bound to rely on the immediate verdicts of uncritical experience: 'Though so little has been attempted, in the way of proof, by those who have treated of our intellectual powers, yet this does not hinder but that we may be, as we unquestionably are, assured, that analogy is of weight in determining our judgement and practice.'
This confidence of Butler's in the verdict of our faculties never fails him, even in that portion of his argument in which he is exhibiting their limitation. Yet here again, as so often, he succeeds in disguising this confidence by the stress that he is forced to lay on the fact that the scheme, whether of Nature or of Revelation, to which they are applied, is a scheme most 'imperfectly comprehended'; and, for that reason, removed out of their judgement. He presses this argument very hard; in a way, no doubt,

that reduces the range of the faculties to a very limited area. But, still, this limitation is never due to distrust in their capacity. The primal authority both of Reason and of Conscience is absolute. No Revelation from God can possibly contradict or override either: for they are the only channels through which a Revelation can reach us. It is impossible to use stronger language than he does on this; and it is strange, indeed, that he should have been misjudged here:—

I express myself with caution lest I should be mistaken to vilify reason, which is, indeed, the only faculty we have wherewith to judge concerning anything, even revelation itself, or be misunderstood to assert that a supposed revelation cannot be proved false from internal characters. For it may contain clear immoralities, and contradictions, and either of these would prove it false (Anal, II. iii. 3).

Again:—

It is the province of reason and conscience to judge of the morality of Scripture, not whether it contains things different from what we should have expected from a wise, just, and good Being, but whether it contains things plainly contradictory to wisdom, justice, and goodness; to what the light of nature teaches us of God.

Now what is the just consequence from all these things? Not that reason is no judge of what is offered to us as being of Divine revelation. For this would be to infer that we are unable to judge of anything, because we are unable to judge of all things. Reason can, and it ought to, judge not only of the meaning, but also of the morality and the evidence of revelation (Anal. II. iii. 26).

And yet again, he reiterates with anxiety, while pleading our incompetence to judge the methods of Revelation:—

This argument is urged, as I hope it will be understood, with great caution of not vilifying the faculty of reason which is 'the Candle of the Lord within us': though it can afford no light where it does not shine, nor judge where it has no principles to judge upon (Anal. II. ix. 7).

For him, the limitations of our faculties are drawn from their knowledge, not from their ignorance; from their exercise, not from their impotence. It is not because the scheme presented to them baffles their power, that they own it to be beyond them. On the contrary, it is because they understand it; and, in understanding it, recognize how much lies beyond what they now cover. They see what they see with perfect validity of judgement; and in seeing it, they see it to be the tiny portion of a larger pattern. They can follow the threads, until they pass out of sight. They are, as it were, looking, and they know it, at a little bit of a picture of which the rest is hidden by a curtain. They see that the colours and curves before their eyes are related to masses and harmonies behind the curtain. The arrangement of colours itself announces this. The curves and lines cry out for that which corresponds and balances. They cannot be understood for what they are, without, at the same time, bearing witness to that which would interpret them, if it were not hidden.

It is not, then, that our faculties fail us; rather, it is their triumphant certainty of apprehension which recognizes the partial character of what is disclosed. It is not the confusion and jumble of what is seen which causes the difficulty; but, on the contrary, its intense coherence, its infinite consistency, its convincing intelligibility. Butler therefore absolutely repudiates the Agnostic argument for our ignorance. If we were wholly without knowledge, we could not say that there was an unknowable world. It is partial ignorance, not total ignorance, from which he argues. For, indeed, 'total ignorance would preclude all argument for or against.' His position is that we know enough of reality to know that we imperfectly comprehend it. It is our knowledge which sets itself its own frontiers by virtue of what it already knows. It knows when it touches its limit; and it knows that what is beyond its present limit is of the same character as that which is within.

And, for that very reason also, Butler finds himself bound to reject the Positivist conclusion, which claims complete knowledge of that which falls inside those limitations. For that which is inside is bound up with that which is outside, as a part is in a whole; and, therefore, it itself cannot be judged and interpreted in isolation. Not only the hidden portion of the picture, but, also, even that little corner of it which our eyes do cover, is therefore beyond our perfect comprehension. For no smallest part can be taken alone. So, out of our knowledge of the part itself, we learn our incapacity to fully estimate it.

Butler thus reaches his characteristic conclusion, that every possible act of knowledge reveals itself as being but partial and incomplete. He defies you to know even this world that lies within our human experience, without knowing something of the world that lies beyond it. For every atom that exists demands the entire Universe to explain it.

No doubt, this is the argument which he drives hardest. While, for instance, asserting the supreme authority of Conscience in moral judgements, he manages to withdraw from the range of its verdict all the particular incidents in the Old Testament that offend, by refusing it the right to pronounce until it knows the ultimate and determining issue. And this it cannot know, without knowing the whole of things in Revelation. Such an argument, so pressed, cannot carry conviction. But it is good, still, to observe that it is the grandeur of his conception of this large coherence in the unity of things, which allows him the use of this argument. It is the immensity of our inheritance which reduces us to silence. It is the splendour of the vision which humiliates, even while it exalts.

And, if he is robust in his optimistic estimate of our human faculties, he is just as dauntless in his outlook on human conduct and human history. And this is all the more noticeable, when we remember how his indignant soul, in its austere passion for righteousness, had nursed a wrathful flame against the thin moral superficialities and cheap benevolence of the literary coteries in Queen Caroline's Salon.

Butler had looked, with serious eyes, into the black abyss of sin; he allowed no easy tolerance to blind him to the turbid disgrace of the story that man had made for himself. He loathed the airy optimism which would not face the fact. Nevertheless, after solemn survey of the whole tumultuous disarray, he deliberately pronounces that all the positive evidence of the facts declares for the right. The underlying principles of Nature are always working for virtue, and against vice. Judged, as they should be, by their tendency, they tally with the verdict of conscience. The spectacle that is presented to us (he pleads) is of a situation in which these tendencies would go much further towards moral perfection, if they were not obstructed. The force for good is there, at work; only it is hampered. If it were given a fair chance, virtue would verify its complete dominion over facts. It would win the whole field to itself. Just as reason has a tendency towards victory so that it will always win where the opportunity is offered it; so there is an essential tendency in virtue to win, and in vice to be beaten. It follows that the positive energies of life have only to be redeemed from hindrances, in order for the ideal kingdom to be attained. Set free the moral forces now at work in human Society; and what more would you need in order to realize the Messianic State? The Ideal, therefore, is already ours in germ and tendency. In its progressive development lies our assured secret of final triumph. So we begin to take the true measure of this vast scheme of one progressive Ideal, moving ever towards its completion, until it embraces the whole sum of things. The ultimate goal is not different in kind from the life that is hid in us here. This life has but to be strengthened and released, and it will be fitted for the perfected state hereafter, towards which we are ever moving.

Here is optimism, indeed. And it is this intense and constructive soundness of his optimistic outlook upon conduct, which leads us, at last, to the cardinal word, so characteristic of the Analogy, and so typically charged with the spirit of Butler—the word 'probation'.

Probation! Somehow, it has a weary and depressing sound. It carries with it to Saxon ears a touch of Latin pedantry and Latin rigidity. It recalls unhappy apologetics, which labour to justify intolerable things by inviting us to suppose that they were all meant for our good.

Yes! There have been intellectual crimes perpetrated in its name. And yet, let us remember that this word, for all its doleful associations, stands for that indomitable optimism in man, which defies all misadventure. It is the expression of man's ineradicable conviction that the world exists for Good, and not for Evil; and that God will ever justify Himself, as victorious over adverse circumstances. Such a conviction, faced by pain and evil, and challenged by the heathen taunt, 'Where is, now, thy God?' bravely retorts by the word 'probation'. It is evil that has happened to us, and not good. We will not play with names, nor call foul fair. But, after all, the evil is there, only to be overcome. It summons us to a field of honour where spurs are to be won. It dares us to give warrant of our worth. In discipline lies the secret of all moral growth; and in hardship the happy warrior recognizes the patent of his nobility. So God asks us to co-operate with Him in wringing good out of evil. He calls upon us to learn a higher obedience, and verify a purer loyalty, through the refining fire of suffering.

So the Jew had answered long ago—the Jew whom Schopenhauer derides for his invincible optimism.

It was no dull affair, this probation, when it threw its meaning out into the splendid Drama of Job. It is not flat, and prosaic, and repellent, as it is poured out in page after page of vehement Prophecy. It escapes, in Isaiah and Jeremiah, far away from the suspicion of apologetic ingenuity, as it tells of the gold that is purged in the furnace, or of the elect servant, who is given over to pain and darkness, that he may emerge with new strength and with heart tested and proved, into the light of a recovered joy.

And once again, in our own day, it has testified to its poetic worth by becoming the ground-motive of one of the very greatest of our Victorian Poets. Robert Browning, in strenuous revolt from Byronic pessimism, set himself to sing the optimistic Creed. And it was under the pressure of this insistent optimism that he found in the idea of spiritual probation the solution of life's darkest mysteries.

We owe it to his genius that the incredible feat should have been accomplished of putting Bishop Butler into verse. Possibly, this may account for some strain and stress in the versification. For it is Butler's favourite type of probation which Browning closely follows. It was Butler who, to justify the logic of probation, argued so convincingly for the possibility of training under one set of conditions a moral character fitted to act under another. It was he who especially gave to probation the ennobling conception of an endless Future, for which this our little day is but a momentary preparation. And this is the familiar theme of which Browning never tires. We are not to ask for perfection here and now? Greek statuary has said the last word on that theme. Old pictures in Florence have another gospel to deliver—the Gospel, not of Time, but of Eternity. Enough if here we just learn the use of the weapons and tools that we shall need hereafter. Enough if we serve our short apprenticeship, and emerge qualified craftsmen. Nothing need, of necessity, be realized on earth. Life is justified, if it has but given us time and opportunity for an equipment, which the

Hereafter will make intelligible.
Things learnt on earth we shall practise in heaven.

For more is not reserved
To man, with soul just nerved
To act to-morrow what he learns to-day:
Here work enough to watch
The Master work, and catch
Hints of the proper craft, tricks of the tool's true play.
Earth changes, but thy soul and God stand sure.
He fixed thee mid this dance
Of plastic circumstance,
This Present, thou, forsooth, wouldst fain arrest:
Machinery just meant
To give thy soul its bent,
Try thee and turn thee forth, sufficiently impressed.
Thou, heaven's consummate cup, what need'st thou with earth's wheel?

All the well-worn passages crowd into our memories.
And it was precisely this relation of Eternity to our probation in the fast-fleeting Present which gave to Butler his constructive power in his own day. The vastness of astronomical times and spaces had bewildered men's sense of proportion, as, for the first time, they apprehended the pettiness of earth over against that immensity of the heavens. The whole scale of knowledge had been widened; and the immediate effect had been to lower the value of anything connected with the discreditable story worked out by humanity 'in an obscure corner of one of the meanest of the planets'. We all know that sudden panic; that dismal shrinkage; that shiver of scorn. Butler encountered it by expanding our human significance. He met the vastness of the physical scheme by disclosing the vastness of the plan of our Redemption. If it requires centuries to unroll the material development, it requires Eternity to complete our spiritual destiny. The Redemptive hope of man is a process, a progress, a growth, extending into the infinite future, far beyond the widest horizons that this surprising science ventures to unveil. And this tiny life here, that seemed to crumple up into nothing under the marvel of those appalling stars, after all, holds in it the secret of endless and immeasurable possibilities, transcending time. Here, in it, lies our probation. Here, in this dim corner, under the discipline of these brief moments, we can be tested for our fitness in a Hereafter which we cannot limit or define. So he enlarged the religious values of life, to meet the heightened demands. He brought our spiritual story up to a level at which it could, courageously and with a recovered self-respect, compete not ingloriously with the majestic revelations of Natural Science.

Probation then had, for him, no dull and tiresome associations. It did not speak of disciplinary pedantries. It told of the joy of a continuous growth from stage to stage of apprenticeship and initiation; of gathering force; of progressive capacities; of daring adventures into the unknown; of prophetic intimations; of the sequence of life upon life, and advance from level to level, through many mansions towards a far-off Divine Event. It meant to him the moral training and equipment for a life of companionship in the transfigured Society, which was to be the consummation of all that draws men together into fertile brotherhood throughout all the long lives of their historic experience. It was of a piece with all that gave to this earthly life its peculiar delight, through its growth out of infancy into childhood, out of childhood into manhood. At every stage, we are under probation for another; and it is this which gives to each stage its importance. In each we have the thrill of feeling that we are acquiring faculties which will have a use far beyond what we can yet imagine. Even in moving through the separate moments of human development here on earth, the poet's cry has its meaning and value:—

Look not thou down but up!
To uses of a cup,...
The Master's lips a-glow.

And this thrill, this prophetic anticipation of unknown achievement, is to be ours, not only for our short space of existence here, but continuously, throughout our whole spiritual career. Religion carries forward the process which Nature has begun.
Let us rehearse his massive summary of this, his high conception. Slowly, as he beats out his thought, the very weight and compass of its movement acquires a certain grandeur of tone:—

It is most obvious, analogy renders it highly credible, that, upon supposition of a moral government, it must be a scheme, system, or constitution, whose parts correspond to each other, and to a whole; as really as any work of art, or of any particular model of a civil constitution and government. In this great scheme of the natural world, individuals have various peculiar relations to other individuals of their own species. And whole species are, we find, variously related to other species, upon this earth.
Nor do we know, how much further these kinds of relations may extend. And, as there is not any action or natural event, which we are acquainted with, so single and unconnected, as not to have a respect to some other actions and events: so possibly each of them, when it has not an immediate, may yet have a remote, natural relation to other actions and events, much beyond the compass of this present work. There seems indeed nothing,

from whence we can so much as make a conjecture, whether all creatures, actions, and events, throughout the whole world of nature, have relations to each other. But, as it is obvious, that all events have future unknown consequences; so if we trace any, as far as we can go, into what is connected with it, we shall find, that if such event were not connected with somewhat further in nature unknown to us, somewhat both past and present, such event could not possibly have been at all.

Nor can we give the whole account of any one thing whatever: of all its causes, ends, and necessary adjuncts; those adjuncts, I mean, without which it could not have been. By this most astonishing connexion, these reciprocal correspondencies and mutual relations, everything which we see in the course of nature is actually brought about. And things seemingly the most insignificant imaginable are perpetually observed to be necessary conditions to other things of the greatest importance: so that any one thing whatever may, for aught we know to the contrary, be a necessary condition of any other (Anal, I. vii. 4-6).

Even in this great passage, we fall under Butler's unfortunate habit of throwing an air of depression over his most inspiring conceptions. For it is brought in to justify his assertion that 'God's moral government must be as much beyond our comprehension as his Nature government suggests'; so that we omit to notice that our ignorance is, itself, the witness to our comprehension of the coherence of the entire Universe in one unbroken and undeviating kingdom which spreads down from the Throne of God to the tiniest atom that falls within the range of Creation. Surely, such a conception ought to carry inspiration with it! Yet he disguises its greatness behind an awkward and melancholy phrase like that of 'a scheme imperfectly comprehended'. He might so easily lighten the effect of this depressing phrase by reminding us that as the scheme would not be known by us to be imperfect unless we were capable of comprehending it, therefore our sense of its imperfection is the measure of our comprehension of its immensity. The stress of the argument, after all, is not on the melancholy fact that we cannot know more, but on the kindling truth that we do know so much. We are inside this scheme that we imperfectly comprehend. That is the great point. We are in actual contact with its reality; and that is why our knowledge of any single object in it cannot be rounded off and completed. If it could, it would prove that we were not knowing the object as it really is: for, in its reality, it cannot be cut off; it cannot be isolated; it cannot be detached from the whole sum of things. The knowledge that isolated it would be knowledge that falsified it.

I venture to repeat this, because it is through recognizing this special character of Butler's attitude towards knowledge that we understand why that in him which is apt to excite a peculiar despair is itself the note of his triumph. For every one is staggered to find Butler arguing that Revelation is full of the same perplexities as Natural Religion; and that Christianity is as imperfectly comprehended as Nature. Yet, if we follow up the lines of his constructive thought, we see, at once, that the very greatness of his conception forced upon him these conclusions. The imperfections that man encounters in his rise from the lower level to the higher will increase rather than diminish; for the rise in thought has admitted him into a scheme of yet vaster proportions than he had hitherto experienced. And, if vaster than the world already within his experience, then, also, it must be still more imperfectly comprehended. The part that falls under his comprehension bears a still smaller proportion than ever to the enormous whole. And the relationships by which it is bound up into the whole are yet subtler and more infinite than any hitherto under his ken. Far, far out of sight the threads pass; far, far away beyond imagination the tendencies press. Man can recognize in them the evidence of their immeasurable reach; and, therefore, he recognizes also that his actual capacity to cover with his knowledge even the corner of it which he can see is more liable than ever to correction from out of a world of which he is even more ignorant than he was of the other world to which his lower experiences belonged. Any rise in real knowledge must, then, involve an extension also in his appreciation of his own ignorance. Revelation, therefore, by virtue of its raising us to a higher level, will display more gaps, more interspaces of ignorance, more moments of baffling perplexity, than did Natural Religion. Christianity, by extending into infinitudes beyond our natural frontiers, will be more charged with bewilderment and uncertainty than Nature. In the one case, as in the other, the imperfections of our comprehension will be bound to recur; and to recur with increasing emphasis, as we move upwards into contact with fuller Reality. Just because it is so far fuller than anything we touch on a lower level, therefore our relationship to it will be more partial and more limited. We shall be less securely aware of how the part stands to the whole, as our estimate of the whole that is out of our sight expands. Revelation, then, does not only fail to clear up the difficulties that Nature has presented to us already; but, leaving them as they were, it adds many more perplexities of its own.

What, then, is the advantage, of a Revelation? For what has it been given? Why should we care to add to our troubles?

Butler's answer is as noble as it is inspiring.

Revelation is simply the call of God to man to 'Come up higher'. If man has shown himself faithful in few things, let him have, as his reward, the fresh responsibility of showing himself faithful in many things. If he can gain five talents in one field, let him prove the like gifts in the higher task of ruling five cities.

This is the law of all spiritual promotion.

And this is the law by which Revelation justifies itself to those who, already, have found evidence for God in Nature. If there, 'mid this dance of plastic circumstance,' man has, in spite of imperfections in his grasp on truth, in spite of all the gaps and interspaces of darkness, yet had the heart and the brain to detect God at work, and to become aware of a vast scheme of ordered and rational good, within which he was to work, and by loyalty to which he was to be judged; then, in response to that loyalty already proved, in recognition of that intellectual and moral insight, let him step up on to a higher plane of existence; let him be admitted to a fuller vision; let him be made aware of yet further action that God has taken on his behalf; let him be brought up into touch with a yet more wonderful scheme of ordered and rational good, by which God has set Himself to redeem all this lower creation into harmony with that divine Consummation of all things in the mystery of Jesus Christ, the Beginning and the End, the Secret Source and the Ultimate Fulfilment of the Purpose and Wisdom which hold all in one.

If there is this fresh development, if God has taken this further action, then, man is under obligation to understand it. For it is a fact; and facts carry with them responsibilities. They open new possibilities; and to refuse to know what these new facts are, is to reject the possibilities opened. So man is laid under probation by a Revelation. To ignore it is to refuse the invitation to come up higher.

Yet the probation imposed by a Revelation will be harder, severer, than any other. It will stretch further the faculties of nerve and brain. It will involve a fiercer strain. For it will ask us to put out a fuller trust in a God who is felt to be hiding Himself in a darkness deeper, often, than any through which Nature has led us. But the temper which held us true to that trust amid the dark vacancies in Nature is the very temper which, under yet stronger strain, will still hold us true to our trust, in the dark places which Revelation itself reveals to be so black. The venture that has been justified on the lower level can, now, justify a more heroic effort; and those who have come thus far on the road must not fear to go yet further. Their courage has so far been proved that it can afford to be set a heavier trial. 'To those that have, is more given;' only, if the finer opportunity is thrown open to them, it will not be at less cost than that which won the lesser prize. The risks to be run will not diminish, the labour and sweat will not slacken, because the reward is higher. Rather, as the Apostle taught us long ago, the discipline grows sharper, as the game passes from the corruptible crown to the incorruptible. The vine that brings forth grapes is, for its honour, pruned with the knife, that it may do yet better.

That is Butler's appeal to us to go forward through Natural Religion to Revelation. These are the motives to which he trusts. Could optimism go further? He grounds himself on man's strength; not on his weakness. He will have nothing to do with those who argue from man's blindness and

Nature's darkness to the necessity for a Revelation to relieve us from impotence and to release us from despair. That is not in the least the way in which the arrival of a Revelation presents itself to him. For him, a Revelation enters in response to those who have eyes to see what Nature has to show them. The light of Revelation, according to his judgement, can only make appeal to those who have already found light on the lower level of natural experience. It enters, not promising to scatter what has been dark; for, indeed, it often leaves (as we find) that which had been dark as baffling as ever. Its main purpose is not to answer riddles that have proved insoluble; but to authorize, sanction, reinforce, and carry forward, the light that already shines. It 're-publishes', in the language of the Analogy, the verities already held. It endows them with stability; it confirms; it reassures. This is its office: and then, secondly, to the light already found, it adds more light; according to the crucial law, that to them who have shall more be given. It opens out new spheres of spiritual experience. It carries man's knowledge forward on to fresh developments. It introduces him to further and fuller activities of God, set in motion on his behalf, for his deliverance.

And, for the apprehension of these new experiences, it asks for just the same moral temper and intellectual insight which have already proved their validity within the narrower frontiers. If these have been hitherto wanting; if Nature has offered to us only a scene of apparent disorder; if the perplexities inevitable in a scheme imperfectly comprehended have staggered our confidence; if we have not had the courage and the patience and the perseverance to detect and to follow the light given us in spite of all the obstacles that hindered its completeness; then, we shall be unequal to the strain of apprehending the Revelation. We shall be baffled by the same objections; we shall be tangled in the like bewilderment. For Revelation must approach us under the same guise and by the same methods. It cannot but make its offer on the same terms. For it, too, cannot but be 'imperfectly comprehended'. It, too, must be obviously incomplete. It will leave, therefore, a thousand issues unresolved. It will be content to prompt, suggest, invite, where certainty is impossible. It will offer partial evidence of just the same type and quality as that which is familiar to us on the plane of Nature. And, if we find it insufficient in the one case, it will seem equally insufficient in the other. In both, its effect will be disciplinary, probational. In both, it will test our moral nerve, and make demands on our spiritual resources. In both, we shall, if we are true to the guidance given us, learn to be grateful for the gaps in our knowledge which testify to the far-reaching wonder of that eternal mystery which we can know only in part. In both, we shall thank God for the incompleteness which bears witness to the splendour of our high citizenship—for the 'fallings from us,' 'the blank misgivings' which tell of that far home from which we came and to which we return.

It would be good, if time allowed, in order to complete our record of Butler's optimism, to touch on his large and liberal use of the analogy of remedial medicine in order to interpret the work of man's Redemption. His fondness for this analogy is a sure indication of his temper: since Remedy is nothing, if it is not optimistic.

For, first, it starts by flinging behind it all the dark problem of 'why' and 'wherefore'. It leaves all this out of account. It will have nothing to do with the question, why this, or that, man is born blind; or why the Tower of Siloam fell on these, and not on those. It is enough for it that the pain is there, and can be healed. Nurses, doctors, leave all else aside; and are absorbed with the hope that, at any rate, they may relieve and cure.

And then, secondly, the idea of Remedy is optimistic, because it assumes that the wrong cannot be meant; cannot be natural; is intended to disappear. Its entire work is based on the conviction that the structure and intention of the organism are sound; that health is the normal condition; that, if only the inner life can be set free to perform its proper functions, the cure will have been effected. Medicine can do nothing, except on this assumption of the inherent and ineradicable rightness of things. Butler's profound confidence in the inherent goodness of things leads him to cling to this illuminating parallel throughout all his treatment of Christ's mediatorial work.

This sure and sturdy confidence in the rightness and reality of facts enables Butler to push off the board a tangle of bewildering perplexities. How can God have given a Revelation, for instance, and yet left it open to mistake, abuse, corruption? Well, why not? He trusts man with splendid natural endowments, and yet takes the risk of their wreckage.

How can you believe that He would bring into play a Revelation which only the few would hear of, and which would have to wait centuries for its opportunities? Well, why not? He has filled earth with treasures and succours, which yet lie hidden century after century, and are only slowly and laboriously discovered and brought into use. He counts on human effort in the one case; why not in the other? Difficulty, struggle, doubt—these are our probation. Through them we have worked out our secular Civilization. Why should not the same methods be equally available in the spiritual sphere? Why should we isolate Religious development from the normal and natural and customary order of things? Why should we imagine for it some special and fantastic dignity, which would forbid it from conforming to our habitual experience?

Again and again, Butler's strong common sense keeps him true and realistic in this way. He is never on stilts. He enjoys common things. He keeps close in touch with things as they are. He goes along with a healthy cheerfulness, resolute in his determination to be loyal to the actual, and to demand no exceptional treatment for Religion or Revelation, as if they lay apart from ordinary human life. Their strength lies in their conformity to natural conditions. The closer their coherence with the common type of human experience and human history, the greater is their reality and the more convincing their evidence. Everything that is most familiar to us in our daily habits reappears in them. They work on the regular lines. That is why we believe in them. Even the very difficulties that recur do but corroborate our confidence by their normality and their familiarity. The two works of Nature and Religion mingle and fuse in one connective continuity of growth.

It would be interesting to follow the working of Butler's mind in detail: but enough has, surely, now been said to suggest how near and intimate is the mind of the man to our own intellectual situation.

For with us, too, as for him, the metaphysical stop is off. Metaphysics are in suspense. The five or six experts who still hand on the good tradition can be heard crying in the night to one another. But no one listens; and they alone understand each other, and carry on faithfully, in a tiny knot, the historic debate on the Existence of the Absolute. Let them hold on to their high faith. Some day their cause will re-emerge. It cannot be that man will ever surrender the heritage won by the heroic endeavour that opened with Plato and closed with Hegel.

But the Vision is not yet. And, in the meantime, we are all anxiously engaged in a debate on the lower plane. We are scientific. We are psychological. We are empirical. We are pragmatic. We are employed, eagerly, in seeing how much can be done without touching on the problems of the higher Logic. We accept the inherent paradoxes of the ultimate Reason. We do not propose to go behind its primary assumptions. We are satisfied with 'transcendental emotion', which allows for no problem, since it has, by its own inherent validity, solved it before it can begin. Or we are content with any formula which can verify its practical efficiency in adapting the facts of life to our dominant interest. Our entire thought is concentrated on Experience. It is the shaping, and the handling, and the assortment of the facts of human Experience with which we are concerned. Even Philosophy has withdrawn from its high a priori methods, and recognizes how intimately its task is set within the challenging limitations of common everyday experience. 'Experience is the beginning and the end of Philosophy,' says a recent philosophic writer. 'Philosophy takes its rise in experience. It is itself a feature in experience. Experience asks the question which philosophy has to answer. In philosophy experience challenges its own validity. Experience is the subject-matter of investigation. Experience is the method of inquiry. The process by which we find out what experience means is itself a form of experience. To the philosopher his philosophy is an experience, i. e. his experience of what experience turns out to be. And this final experience of the philosopher, which is his philosophy, returns for verification to the experience of the ordinary man from out of which it arose' (Richmond, Essay on Personality, ch. i. p.4. Arnold).

In that forcible passage we feel the intensity which the modern development of Thought has thrown into our direct, personal experience. There, or nowhere, we are in face of all that can be known. So we all recognize. And we shall do so with ever-growing directness. Metaphysic itself, when it comes again to its own, will do so by verifying, with a closer intimacy than ever, its inevitable inherence within the very heart's core of our common average experience.

And it is within this human experience of ours that Butler does all his work. It is our daily Experience that he fastens on, clings to, accepts. For him, it holds the entire secret. He has no desire to go behind it, or beyond it. It is sufficient. It justifies itself. It supplies the standard to which reality must conform. It contains and reveals the main method by which truth discloses itself. He takes his ground on it. He starts with it. He ends with it, or with what it suggests and sanctions. We have but to examine, he thinks, the mode in which facts of daily experience commend themselves to us, and we shall be in possession of the conditions which determine the arrival of the Truth, whether through Nature or Revelation.

We have no power except through the facts. He distrusts profoundly, not reason, but the uninstructed reason—the reason that draws its knowledge out of itself. Reason has nothing of its own to draw upon. It is, itself, the faculty to know facts; and, in knowing facts, it carries with it its own guarantee. It knows them as they are meant to be known. So Butler's appeal is ever from the reason uninformed by experience to the reason which has accepted the facts set before it—from the reason e. g. which decrees what a Revelation must involve, to the reason which will be content to understand what a Revelation, in fact, actually is. He will never refuse facts, nor ever leave them behind. At every stage the reason is recalled by him to the actual verdict of experience.

This may compel Butler, as it does, to enforce the strictness of the limitations under which reason works; for it cannot go beyond what the facts that lie within its experience will justify. And that experience is very partial. And the facts are imperfectly comprehended.

But the very limitations that he enforces are not imposed from without; nor are they incidental to some formal insufficiency of reason itself. They spring up out of the very nature of experience itself. They are asserted by virtue of the facts themselves, which, in being known as what they are, declare themselves to be but partially known. The limitations come, not from any defects in our intellectual organs, but from the evident and undeniable narrowness of the area over which they have, as yet, been exercised.

There is, therefore, optimism, still, even in the recognition of limitation.

Our capacities only need the widening of their area of exercise, to prove themselves adequate to new knowledge. And there need be no limit to this expression of their experience. Life is a perpetual progress in experience. And our knowledge, therefore, has, before it the vision of limitless growth. In all this, Butler shows himself the friend of the scientific temper which has become the dominant element in the modern mind. His certitude is the scientific certitude in the sure value of facts and faculties, which is so victoriously robust that it can absolutely afford to disregard the criticism of metaphysics.

The limitations which he emphasizes are the limitations which Science emphasizes, as the inevitable conditions of the confined area to which our petty human experience is confined; while the compensating promise of endless advance in knowledge has in it the very note of scientific confidence.

The overriding Authority, for which Butler pleads, is the authority with which Science makes such dread play—the authority of stern unbending facts, and of the urgent pressure of past action; the authority expressed through the famous phrase, 'Things are what they are, and their consequences will be what they will be;' while the qualifications and corrections which can be brought to bear upon the necessities created by the Past take the scientific form of Remedy, which accepts the facts, and empowers them to rid themselves of their own poison and to work out their own cure.

So, again, the whole theology of Rewards and Punishments is identified by Butler with the sequence in Nature of Cause and Effect, flushed by the influng transfiguration of a divine intention. Thus, at every point, he lays himself alongside of the scientific temperament, and tallies with its outlook.

In throwing this mystical intensity into the experiential presentation of the world which is given through Natural Science, Butler had behind him the support of the Wisdom Literature with which he was so intimately in alliance. For there, too, the Vision of Truth which was so ardently pursued was no high metaphysic of the Absolute. The writers use language of such spiritual exaltation that we fancy ourselves to be engaged in some Platonic communion with the Idea of Intellectual Beauty. This Wisdom 'is more beautiful than the sun, and above all the order of the stars. She is the breath of the power of God, and a pure influence flowing from the glory of the Almighty. She is the brightness of the everlasting light, the unspotted mirror of the power of God, and the image of His goodness' (Wisd. vii). Yet, when we ask what it is which so enthralls its possessor, it turns out to be singularly concrete and near and practical. It is, he tells us, the power to 'know how the world was made, and the operation of the elements: the alterations of the turning of the sun, and the change of seasons: the circuits of years, and the positions of stars: the natures of living creatures, and the furies of wild beasts: the violence of winds, and the reasonings of men: the diversities of plants, and the virtues of roots: and all such things as are either secret or manifest' (Wisd. vii). Wisdom has shown him, moreover, that 'the principal things for the whole use of man's life are water, fire, iron, and salt, flower of wheat, honey, milk, and the blood of the grape, and oil, and clothing' (Ecclus. xxxix). Herein lies his intellectual delight. It is Natural Science that is his mistress. Knowledge is, for him, above all things progressive. It draws all things one way, according to a practical determination of the will; it goes through from end to end, sweetly ordering all things. It makes of the universe a co-ordinate scheme which can only be understood in its entire sum. All is allotted, measured, fixed, correlated. Each minute detail finds its own peculiar justification by virtue of its coherent relationships, working out to the one harmonious consummation. This is his Ideal of Truth, and it is obviously Butler's also.

And so, too, for this ancient philosophy, the Ideal presented in the sphere of Nature is identical with the moral Ideal. This Wisdom ordereth a man's life according to the same law by which it determines all else. The moral law is the human equivalent of the coherence which knits the universe into unity of purpose; and this same Wisdom, which teaches the circuits of the sun, gives to the man, into whose soul it enters, knowledge of judgement and law, by 'which to frame his life in righteousness, and to execute judgement with an upright heart. She leads him soberly in all his ways; so that his works are acceptable, and he is worthy to sit in his father's seat'.

Butler would delight in bringing the moral life of humanity into this complete accord with the conception of Natural Law. He would have the same confidence in asserting that 'the fear of the Lord—that is wisdom; and to depart from evil—that is understanding'.

Would he imply that all Truth is purposive, and that Thought is only an expression of Will—an organ of Selection?

We are forcing matters by putting such questions to him. He had not such an issue before him. Metaphysic held too paramount a throne for her whole existence to be thus roughly challenged. Butler never doubts her prerogative. Only, he had other interests than hers. He is entirely content to work on what are to her probabilities. He is satisfied with a mode of knowledge by analogy, which is eminently practical; and he has no leisure to examine the logical principles on which the authority of such knowledge must be based.

Sometimes, no doubt, in his scorn for the uninstructed reason he may seem to use language which would deny the validity of all knowledge that was merely critical and dialectical. But, after all, he is only dealing with reason in its treatment of experience; and there he is right in claiming that facts are everything, and presupposition nothing.

So, again, in his examination of Determinism, he can fitly excuse himself from sounding its speculative depths, since, for his purpose, it is enough that, practically, we must act as if we were free.

He has no real occasion to go beyond the frontiers of empirics; and he is glad to take advantage of this limitation. Within these frontiers knowledge is always purposive. It is the exhibition of the real coherence of things in an effective adaptation to a unity of Purpose. On the other hand, Butler gave a universal value to the verdicts of Conscience and Reason, whenever these were in possession of the facts. He never regarded these faculties as mere expressions of an individual mood. He assumes that their standard has an identity of its own, which does not vary with the experiences to which it is applied. It would be impossible for him to picture reason as merely a sensitive tentacle by which an individual organism pushes its way forward into effective co-operation with its environment.

Is he not, then, one of us? Does he not reflect our own familiar hesitations and limitations? Is he not of our own time and range? We, too, are feeling the full force of these practical values which determine our thinking. We, too, recognize the purposive character of our ordinary intellectual schematization. We, too, are vividly aware of the strange variety of accumulated influences which enter into our practical judgements, and how delicate and manifold a business it is to weigh out, in balances, the forces that, out of a mass of half-conscious experience, focus themselves finally into a verdict.

Who can give to these determinants any fixed logical rule of valuation? What dialectical arithmetic is equal to the subtlety of these calculations? Can we follow the movement of reason to its conclusion, any more than we can track the flight of a bird through the air that closes behind it as it passes? And can we distribute the weight of individual progression, or discount the personal equation?

There are probabilities of every range and scale; probabilities within probabilities. And the intellectual effect that they produce can only be accounted for through the delicacies and intricacies of psychological analysis. And, moreover, there is an unsounded subconscious world pushing upward, by irruption and invasion, and making its own disturbing contribution to the result. So we learn; so we feel; so we know. And Butler would have entered with zest into all this novel psychology of our day, and would have revelled in exhibiting the selective fertility with which our experience created its own values out of the qualities of its moral character and purpose.

And yet Bishop Butler would not, I think, have disguised from himself the fact that this success in estimating truth according to the measure of its practical efficiency is won by confining attention to a limited area within recognized frontiers. It leaves ultimate issues unresolved. It can afford to go on its way without touching them, but it knows that they are there, and will, ultimately, emerge. Butler is aware that a critical examination of the logical values of his argument from analogy is waiting for him in the background, however 'natural and just and conclusive' it is in its practical working. He would know that, finally, the debate would push home its inquiry into the character of those frontiers which it had been content to assume. It would be bound to pass criticism on itself: to challenge the validity of its own experience: to transcend the dualism which experience assumes, and to discover a monism in which both factors found their reconciliation. If knowledge be purposive, yet there must be a criterion of purposes: there must be a distinction in the reality of purposes: there must be an ultimate standard by which to determine what constitutes the truest form of practical efficiency. The knowledge may be symbolic, but the symbols must be graded; and they must be ever approaching nearer to the perfect expression in which the whole of reality is ultimately uttered. After all, we believe in 'the Word that was with God'. These is a Word which is adequate to its function. There cannot be for ever 'the something over' that is unexpressed.

The ultimate problem remains, that is; and the last word of all will still have to be discovered, when all that can be wrung out of psychological and practical valuations has been completed. Butler would not deny this, I would plead, even though he will not seriously concern himself over this ultimate problem, and has little to suggest about it. His own work, his own impressiveness, are done and won in other fields: and those fields are ours, and are at our very doors. In those same fields we toil and moil, labouring to reduce our bewildering mass of experience to effective order and coherency—labouring to read the secret by which it may be handled with practical efficiency and security of purpose. It might, surely, be an immense relief to us, under the storm and stress of our tremendous task, to have by our side, a fellow worker who sets himself resolutely to our particular business: who is determined to accept every conceivable fact that experience can bring him: who faces all that man is called upon to face, however vast and appalling, however strange and unanticipated, however repellent and grim: and who still emerges confident and self-possessed, utterly convinced of the rightness that is at the root of things, and of the worth of man's conscience and of the validity of man's reason: sure of the light that he follows, of its sufficiency for life's purpose, of its adequacy for all future emergencies, of its power to expand under the gradual advance by which man moves ever onwards from level to level, from task to task, in answer to a voice that invites him to come up higher.

This man, so serious, so anxious, so open-eyed, so relentlessly candid, so deliberate, so reasonable, so real, so unflinchingly true to the facts as they actually are, yet issues out of his long wrestle in the night, possessed of a Vision which never fails him. It holds, for him, the entire Universe together in a coherent and progressive Purpose, stretching from the lowest point of physical existence, through all the grades of Natural Development, up to the highest order of the Spiritual Heaven disclosed to us through the open door of Revelation. One secret makes itself known everywhere: one mind is everywhere reiterating its tireless delight: one pressure sets everywhere towards one far-off event. And into this Vision man is, in his measure, admitted. He can already follow its traces; and according to the faithfulness and love, patience, and courage with which he pursues it amid the perplexities that encumber and beset his path, he proves his fitness to receive more and more of its growing light. Step by step, he may rise; and still he learns the better use of his faculties and the finer qualities of his craft. If only he will learn, and not dictate; if only he will open out to the instruction of experience, and not strive to impose his own presumption on the facts as they arrive: then, the possibilities before him are inexhaustible. Through time, and through eternity, he will live according to the one law, in obedience to a single process, moving on from glory to glory, in the face of Jesus Christ. The greatness of the glory revealed will, no doubt, as it makes its immensity felt, demand of him an ever-growing recognition of the little that he can cover under his own experience, and of the limitless mystery that lies beyond, elusive and 'imperfectly comprehended'. This necessity will ever demand that his advance in knowledge should carry with it an ethical discipline, shaping a moral character which can endure the limitations incident to such exaltation. The temper that is given in and through Christ can alone suffice to the attainment of this high knowledge. Reason and Religion are, therefore, at one; moral and intellectual growth coincide.

This is Butler's Gospel. This is the optimism to which he attained through much tribulation. It is a Gospel that would have commended itself, I am sure, to him whose dear memory is honoured, and preserved to Oxford, by the title of this Lecture. Is there any intellectual Gospel that will more aptly meet our needs, under the strain of a day like our own, darkened by much depression, loaded with heavy burdens, beset with unanticipated bewilderment, and yet conscious of a great hope labouring towards its fulfilment—of a light that can be felt behind the clouds?

As we recall this strong and inspiring argument, we see how entirely it escapes from falling under the ordinary criticism of the Analogy, such as is given, in its most vivid shape, in the following passage from Mr. Bagehot's Essay on Bishop Butler:—

Let us look at the argument more at length. The supposition and idea of a "miraculous revelation" rest on the ignorance of man. The scene of nature is stretched out before him; it has rich imagery, and varied colours, and infinite extent; its powers move with a vast sweep; its results are executed with exact precision; it gladdens the eyes, and enriches the imagination; it tells us something of God—something important, yet not enough. For example, difficulties abound; poverty and sin, pain and sorrow, fear and anger, press on us with a heavy weight. On every side our knowledge is confined and our means of enlarging it small. Of this the outer world takes no heed; Nature is "unfeeling"; her laws roll on; "beautiful and dumb," she passes forward and vouchsafes no sign. Indeed, she seems to hide, as one might fancy, the dark mysteries of life which seem to lie beneath; our feeble eyes strain to look forward, but her "painted veil" hangs over all, like an October mist upon the morning hills. Here, as it seems, revelation intervenes; God will break the spell that is upon us; will meet our needs; will break, as it were, through the veil of nature; He will show us of Himself. It is not likely, surely, that He will break the everlasting silence to no end; that, having begun to speak, He will tell us nothing; that He will leave the difficulties of life where He found them; that He will repeat them in His speech; that He will revive them in His word. It seems rather, as if His faintest disclosure, His least word, would shed abundant light on all doubts, would take the weight from our minds, would remove the gnawing anguish from our hearts. Surely, surely, if He speaks He will make an end of speaking, He will show us some good, He will destroy "the veil that is spread over all nations", and the "covering over all people"; He will not "darken counsel by words without knowledge"' (Bagehot, Literary Studies, vol. ii. p. 83. Longmans).

It will now be seen that this passage starts on exactly the assumption which Butler repudiates. It supposes that the intervention of a Revelation is due to man's ignorance; and has for its purpose the removal of the doubts raised by Nature. But to Butler, Revelation is the reward given to man's knowledge; and its purpose is, not to solve old enigmas, but to lead him upward to new truths. Revelation offers to man this inspiring invitation: 'Thou hast been faithful in little. Be faithful also in much.'

www.ingramcontent.com/pod-product-compliance
Lightning Source LLC
Chambersburg PA
CBHW061936280526
45787CB00004B/1629